mindfulness **for kids**

mindfulness
for kids

30 fun activities
to stay calm,
happy & in control

Carole P. Roman and
J. Robin Albertson-Wren

ALTHEA
PRESS

Interior Designer: Liz Cosgrove
Cover Designer: Amy King
Editor: Melissa Valentine
Production Editor: Andrew Yackira

Author photography © Owen Kassimir (Carole) and © Melissa Conley (Robin).
Illustrations: © Sam Kalda, 2018.

ISBN: Print 978-1-64152-085-0
eBook: 978-1-64152-327-1

R1

For David

You can't stop the waves,
but you can learn to surf.
—Jon Kabat-Zinn

(CPR)

For every child around the world,
working to gain self-awareness,
resiliency, and compassion.

(JRAW)

contents

part two:
how to be a mindful you at school 25

part three:
how to be a mindful you
with friends

a letter to grown-ups

Dear Caregiver,

Thank you for your interest in this mindfulness book for kids.

More and more research supports the profound and positive effects that mindfulness strategies can have on our children. As we would train our bodies for any athletic endeavor, we can also build the muscle in our brains, enabling us to strengthen and develop the decision-making parts of our minds, enhance our memory and recall abilities, and subdue the "fight, flight, or freeze" response that was useful for our ancestors but can get us into trouble around the dinner table or in the parking lot.

In my years of training as a mindfulness instructor, I have worked with children ages 3 to 17 who, through regular practice, demonstrate positive changes in their abilities to pay attention, remember and recall information, self-regulate their behavior, feel more confident, and act with kindness and compassion toward their peers. I'm delighted to share these exercises and tips with you and those dear to you.

In this book, you'll read stories in which kids find themselves in situations where they need to call on a skillful choice. Alongside those stories, you'll find many techniques that I have found useful in my classroom and in private practice with clients. These techniques are shared through the voices of five children: Jasmine, Willow, Kayli, Colby, and Zeke, who show up repeatedly to share their own mindfulness exercises as strategies to use in a variety of difficult situations. The stories in this book are easy to relate to, and children will find they identify with many of the characters and their multitude of emotions. Enjoy these 15 different stories and their corresponding mindfulness exercises. Read this book aloud or side-by-side with the children in your life. Practice some of these exercises and techniques, bookmark your favorites, and return to them often.

Here's to joining a growing number of families who are searching for ways to gain greater awareness, self-control, resiliency, and compassion!

Fondly,
J. Robin Albertson-Wren

a letter to kids

Dear Young Reader,

   Welcome, friend! This book has been created just for you. It's actually a storybook, with many tales about kids and the challenges they face. But it's also full of ideas and activities that you can try at home, at school, and out in the world.

   You'll hear from lots of kids who get into tough situations and who need some help handling their emotions. You'll learn what mindfulness is, and how it can help. You'll also meet five kids who really know a lot about mindfulness—and they offer their helpful suggestions! Jasmine, Willow, Kayli, Colby, and Zeke are your mindfulness guides, and they show up in this book over and over to share mindfulness exercises that helped them deal with their own difficult emotions. Their activities will help you practice exploring how you can be the "best you," even when things seem hard.

We all have fun emotions, like happy, excited, surprised, and proud. We also have some not-so-fun emotions, like angry, sad, frustrated, and upset. Every day, we feel a mixture of many different emotions. The positive ones are fun to hang on to, but the negative feelings sometimes feel like they are holding on to *us*.

Have you ever felt angry or sad, and you feel like it ruined your whole day? Mindfulness can help us become aware of our feelings and experience them without letting them control us.

Read and enjoy the stories in this book. Pretend you're a part of them. I wonder where you might see yourself in each story. Then, experiment with the exercises and see which ones work best for you. Bookmark your favorites and return to them whenever you want. Now, let's get mindful!

With love and hugs,
J. Robin Albertson-Wren

mindfulness:
what's that?

"Mindfulness" is a big word, but it's really easy to understand. It just means paying attention to what's happening **right now**. You can be mindful by using one or all of your senses—sight, sound, taste, smell, and feel.

Mindfulness of **sight** is when you pay attention to what you see using your eyes.

You can be mindful of **sound**, perhaps noticing sounds that are loud or soft, or very far away, or very close to you. Have you ever closed your eyes when you have tasted something delicious? You are being mindful. That's you zooming in on **taste** right then! When you notice a certain aroma and you smile or wrinkle your nose, you are being mindful of **smell**. Even when you're really busy, you can be aware of how things **feel**, noticing textures like scratchy or smooth, soft or hard. You can pay attention to warmth or cold.

Most importantly, you can be mindful of what is going on inside of you, with your **emotions**. This means recognizing when you are growing angry or sad or worried. This is the part of mindfulness we will really explore. As you practice paying attention to your emotions, you can even begin to notice where you feel these emotions in your body!

Okay, now the tricky part. Mindfulness is doing all this noticing **without judging**. When you practice mindfulness, you can treat everything like an experiment. See what you notice. Like, "Ahh, I'm really comfortable and my breath is deep and slow" or "Hey, I'm feeling mad, and my hands are clenched into fists." When you are aware of what your body is doing, you can take steps to fix it and feel better.

When you realize what is going on around you (in your environment) and inside of you (with your emotions), you can feel more in control. You can choose which behavior you want to use. When you make your *own* decisions, you're likely to feel happier and make better choices. This book will help you become a "Mindful You"—the one who makes the best choices even when things get tough!

Try the exercises in this book to help in difficult or upsetting situations. The more practice you have becoming mindful, the more aware and in control you'll feel. Get ready to welcome the Mindful You!

part one

how to be a mindful you at home

STORY 1

jayden loses his phone, *again*

"Where is your phone?" Mom asked, looking mad. Jayden tore through his backpack trying to find it. His math workbook split apart at the seams and slipped onto the floor.

"Jayden! Be careful!" She snatched the workbook from the floor and placed it on the table. "I thought we talked about being more mindful about your belongings. Do you know how much we paid for that phone?"

"I know, Mom," Jayden said. He dumped the rest of the contents on the table, where the pile grew like an erupting volcano.

Mom walked over and with two fingers picked a few scattered papers from the mess. One sheet had a peppermint candy left over from the holiday party stuck to it. She held the fuzz-covered candy over the trash and flicked it in.

"When was the last time you cleaned your bag? You're supposed to do it at the end of each week."

Jayden opened his mouth to say something. He could lie and say it was a new assignment, but he knew by looking at the disaster on the table she would smell it out in an instant so he kept quiet.

"I don't see it here," Mom said, looking disappointed. "Where is your phone?"

Jayden looked at the floor, then at the ceiling. He looked everywhere but at her face. He felt the heat rise to his cheeks and couldn't talk even if he had an answer. The words were stuck in his throat.

"I don't know, Mom," Jayden said, a little too loudly. "I put it in there!" he said, pointing to his book bag. His breath came in short bursts. "I put it in there," he repeated, as he wiped away a tear from his eye. He was really angry with himself, but he wouldn't cry. He just wouldn't.

zeke's tools to ease anger and frustration

feather flutter breathing

When I feel mad or upset, I try to pay attention to my breathing. This helps me calm down. I found a feather that I keep near my bed. When I get mad, the feather helps me, with a trick I call feather flutter breathing. First, I hold the feather in front of my face and notice how my fast, ragged breath moves the feather back and forth. As I try to take deeper, slower breaths in and out, the feather's movements turn to gentle flutters. When I feel better, I take a deep breath in and hold the feather high. Then I let the feather go and try to make my out-breath last until the feather lands softly on my bed.

count to calm

Sometimes counting helps me calm my thoughts when I am frustrated. Here's how: I close my eyes and breathe in through my nose. Then I breathe out through my mouth. In and out counts as one breath. I breathe this way 10 times, concentrating the whole time on the air going in and out.

It's kind of fun to challenge myself. I like to try different ways of counting. Usually, I start counting by 1s to 10, but then I might try it again by 5s or 3s to 30 or even higher. Try it and see what works for you.

STORY 2

no fair! everyone's playing but sophie

"It's not fair." Sophie drummed her fingers on the windowsill. All the other kids were outside. Her lower lip trembled. She heard the shouts as they ran down the street.

Brian, her younger brother, had already fed the dog and was outside having fun. Why did *she* have to take out the garbage? Why couldn't her job be feeding the dog?

She heard the clatter of pots and knew Dad was preparing dinner. "Sophie!" he yelled. "The trash is full! You have to take it out!"

Sophie dashed a hand in front of her stinging eyes. None of her friends had to help with stinky things like taking out the garbage.

Her dad called again, but Sophie ignored him. She hated doing that chore. She had to empty *every can* in the house! Sometimes

7

goopy things fell out of the trash, making a mess on the floor. All Brian had to do was pour a cup of kibble into Grover's dish and put fresh water in the other bowl. Anger made her scalp feel tight. She bit her bottom lip.

"Soph," Dad stuck his head in the door of her bedroom.

Sophie balled up her fists. Her eyes squinted and her face grew flushed. It's not that she didn't want to help Dad. *Why did it have to be the garbage?* "Why can't *I* feed the dog and Brian take out the trash?" she whined, throwing herself on the bed. "It's too hard," she moaned into her pillow. "I can't do it!"

Her father didn't respond; he just raised one eyebrow. "Five-minute warning," he said, walking out of the room. Sophie stared at the ceiling. She felt her cheeks grow hot, and a tear leaked from the corner of her eye. She pressed her hands to her face. "It's not fair!" she hissed under her breath.

kayli's ideas for handling frustration and resentment

trading places

When I feel resentful toward a grown-up, I try to imagine that I am the grown-up and they are me. I go to a quiet space and close my eyes, then picture myself as the grown-up. Sometimes I picture how great it would be to be the boss. But then I keep imagining, and I see myself having to remind someone else over and over to help with chores. I feel frustrated then, too. I start to see how people's actions affect other people. I can grow kinder and more thoughtful when I think about how my choices might make other people feel. Thinking about how others feel makes me feel less resentful.

self-reflection

Sometimes when I have projects or chores, I get frustrated because I won't have time for all the other fun stuff I was hoping to do. It's hard to get chores done quickly when my brain is full of angry thoughts. I do this simple trick to calm myself down: I look in the bathroom mirror. Sometimes my squinched-up mad face makes me laugh out loud, and I begin to calm down. If my face isn't mad enough, I make the maddest face I can. Now I'm really laughing. When I feel calmer, I think better, and now I can get my jobs done quickly and then go play.

STORY 3

bad breaks!
max and justin
shatter a mirror

Max bounced on his parents' bed, waving a pillow at his brother.
"That didn't count," he shouted.

"Yes, it did. I got you right in the face," Justin responded.

"No you didn't," Max laughed, playfully hitting him on the head.
Justin exploded in laughter, which filled the room.

"I'll get you!" Closing his eyes, Justin pushed the pillow at him.

"You're too slow." Max easily dodged him. Justin wasn't sure
how it happened; it could have been when they bounced together
on the bed, striking each other at the same time. The pillow flew
from his hands, hitting the mirror over their parents' dresser.

"No!" he held both hands out in front of him as it teetered on its
base, then crashed into a million pieces on the floor.

"Oh!" Justin shouted. "What are we going to do?" For a minute he couldn't breathe, then he gulped a breath through a sob. He clutched his brother's arm, his stomach quivering nervously. They were going to get in *so much trouble*.

Justin's heart was beating like a trapped bird in his chest. His hands shook as if he were freezing. He saw a portion of his scared face in a sliver of glass. He didn't recognize himself; his eyes were wide with fright. He shivered. This was bad. Mom and Dad would be angry, but this would be a level beyond what they'd experienced before.

"It's even worse than it looks," Justin muttered. His jaw felt tight, and his shoulders felt frozen, his arms were locked against his sides. He looked at his brother, the words rasping in his throat. "Grandma told me breaking a mirror brings bad luck."

"That's just a silly superstition," Max assured him with a shaky voice.

 ## colby's ideas for handling guilt and overwhelm

freeze-frame

Just like when Max and Justin broke their parents' mirror, I freeze up when I've done something wrong. When I feel guilty about something, I keep my body as still as possible and do a quick "mental body scan" to get my negative thoughts back in line—and you can, too! Notice your feet on the floor and the position of your arms and hands. Then pay attention to your shoulders and your jaw. See how tight they are. Then loosen your muscles, wiggle your body, shake your hands, open your mouth as if you are going to yawn, and shrug your shoulders. Once you loosen up a bit, you can make a plan to fix the mistake.

muscle movement

Have you ever felt like you're going to burst and your body just *has* to move? When I'm upset or excited, I try to pay attention to what my muscles need. I like to go outside and run around in giant circles, stretching my legs and pumping my arms and taking in big gulps of air and breathing out in quick little bursts. As my body gets tired, I make my running circles smaller and my exhales longer. By the time I stop, my exhales are lasting longer than my inhales and I can feel my mind and my body settling.

mindfulness and your brain

colby's lesson: how mindfulness helps your brain

When we practice mindfulness, it can make us feel more aware. But it also makes us feel more peaceful and in control. I think it's really cool to learn a little bit about mindfulness and our brains! We have three areas of our brains that mindfulness can help.

The first is the **amygdala**. That's the emotional control center of our brains. It's located right at the base of our brain stem, in the back of our head, near where it meets the neck. That's the part of our brain that takes over when we get upset—where our "fight, flight, or freeze" response is stored.

Have you ever heard that elephants have a great memory? Well, the **hippocampus** (sounds like another zoo animal, right?) is the part of our brain that stores memories and information.

And the **prefrontal cortex**, right behind our forehead, is the highest-level thinking part of our brains—where we plan and make decisions.

How does mindfulness help these brain parts? Well, mindfulness exercises help strengthen our hippocampus and prefrontal cortex. These parts actually grow, just like the muscles in your legs when you run playing soccer. And you can train your brain! Mindfulness exercises help the amygdala (holding your angry, frustrated, or jealous feelings) shut off and activate the hippocampus (the memory part) and the prefrontal cortex (the smart part) so you can recall information, make healthy decisions, and choose a more thoughtful response to any situation. Mindfulness practice helps you program your own brain so you can react better. Awesome, right?

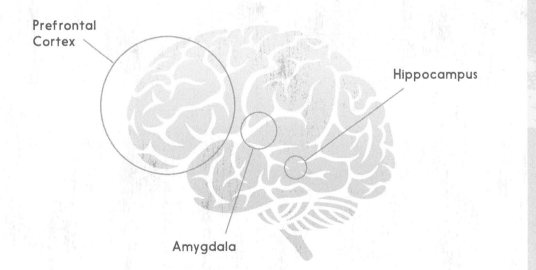

Prefrontal Cortex

Hippocampus

Amygdala

STORY 4

battle over the remote

Mia's mom was busy preparing a presentation for work. "Would you mind reading in the other room, honey? I need some quiet," her mom said.

"Can we go for ice cream afterward?" Mia asked.

Her mother smiled. "Sure." Mia skipped to the den. Her older brother, Nicolas, was on the couch reading. Mia curled up in the cozy chair and opened her book.

Suddenly, the television sprang to life, the sound filling the room. Mia looked up. Nicolas was watching TV. "Shut it off. We're supposed to be reading," she told him. Nicolas ignored her.

Mia raised her voice, "Shut off the TV, or we won't be able to go for ice cream later."

Nicolas acted as if he didn't hear her. Mia stomped to the couch to grab the remote. Nicolas blocked her from it, holding it tightly behind him. Mia exhaled a deep breath. *Nicolas is going to make us miss ice cream, just like he did last week*, she thought.

She opened her mouth to call her mom, then snapped it shut. She clenched her hands, her body quivering. "Give it to me."

Nicolas just smirked, and Mia's shoulders went rigid. She really wanted that ice cream, and Nicolas was not going to screw things up again. She whispered fiercely. "Give it back."

Gritting her teeth, she reached for the remote, but Nicolas held it high. She heard herself groaning as she tried to grab it. "Is everything okay?" her mother called. Mia went silent. She worried the noise would anger her mother, and then there would be no treat. She struggled with her brother as quietly as she could; their grunts filled the room. In the struggle for the remote, the sound blasted from the speaker. "Lower the volume," her mom called.

Nicolas laughed. Mia threw herself on the sofa. Her hands were fidgeting, and she wanted to scream. "You ruined everything," she said to her brother. "Now we won't get ice cream."

jasmine's ideas to reset your body and mind

six-count breaths

Other people can make you so mad sometimes, right?! When I feel my temperature rising and I get all hot in my face, when I notice my fists clenching and I can't think straight, I do six-count breaths. Here's how: I fling myself down on the couch and breathe big, deep breaths. I count to four and feel the air going in. I hold my breath for two seconds and then let my breath out super slowly, counting to six in my head. Breathing in and breathing out, big and slow, my heart rate slows, and that sends a chemical message to my brain that I'm relaxed. I can start to think again, and now I can think of a plan.

breathing kindness

It can be hard to act kind when I am mad at someone. In this activity, I close my eyes and picture that person (for example, my brother) doing something he loves. I picture his whole room, his clothes, and all his stuff. He might be smiling or laughing. I take 10 breaths, and at the beginning of the first one I whisper, "May you be happy." I breathe a second time and picture him being happy. On my third breath, I say, "May you be healthy." On my fourth breath, I picture him being healthy. I continue with other kind wishes: "May you believe in yourself." "May you stay safe." "May you feel peaceful." Ten breaths of kindness, and now I'm not so mad at him!

STORY 5

doctor's office panic

"Hurry, Dan. You have an appointment with Doctor Harrison."

"What?" Daniel asked, suddenly tense.

Mom glanced at the clock. "You have a school checkup."

"Wait, Mom," Daniel began. "Do I have to go?" He gulped and asked, "It's just a checkup, right?"

"Please finish your dinner, Daniel," his mother said.

Daniel dropped his fork; it clattered noisily against his plate. "I'm not getting a needle, right? No needles." He looked up at his mother worriedly.

"Well, Dan," Mom said calmly. "This is your second-grade checkup. If I remember correctly, there is a booster this year . . . Mumps, I think."

Daniel took a deep breath. He kicked the legs of his chair, his face glum. "I don't want to get a shot."

"It'll be fine, Son," Dad said. Daniel said nothing and moved the meat around on his plate without eating anything. He knew it would taste like sawdust in his mouth anyway. He drank a big sip of water; he was so thirsty. Nerves made his mouth drier than dust.

Mom started clearing the table. "Come on, we're running late." Daniel's stomach clenched. For a minute he was afraid he'd throw up. He hated sitting in the office while the doctor filled the needle. Then there was that cold cotton ball and that moment of wondering when the doctor would jab your arm. Daniel shivered and put his fork down. He wasn't hungry anymore. He couldn't eat anything else. He shoved himself from the table; his chair tilted dangerously.

"Daniel!" his mother warned.

"I don't wanna go," he wailed loudly, sweat beading on his brow. The kitchen was filled with the sound of Daniel's rising voice. He put his head on the table, moaning, his hands clutching his stomach. "I don't wanna go. My belly hurts." He felt his belly flutter like it was full of a bunch of little butterflies.

 willow's advice on handling fear and anxiety

feet on the ground

When I feel scared, it's usually because I don't know what to expect. This fear and worry create awful stories in my mind. To help myself calm these emotions, I stop and pay attention to my body. I notice my feet on the ground. I start to walk, taking slow, thoughtful steps. I notice my footsteps grounding me to the earth. I become aware of each foot lifting and how my heels touch the floor. I feel the pavement or carpet or floor beneath me and how it feels on the pads of my feet. Taking five slow steps, first to the left, then turning and taking another five to the right, I begin to feel more grounded.

tune in

When I stop and listen to everything around me, I can help myself slow down. This exercise helps me focus *before* I react to something that bothers me. If you are feeling anxious, try this: Pause for a moment, wherever you are, and tune in to your ears. Focus on a sound that is far away. Stay with it, listening to that one sound until it changes or disappears. Then try listening to another sound close to you, maybe even the sound of your own quiet breathing. What's the loudest sound you notice? The quietest? How many different sounds can you hear? And are you calmer now?

part two

how to be a mindful you at school

STORY 6

presentation panic!

Kevin was telling a story about his trip to New York. The whole class was laughing at the funny parts. Stewart squirmed in his seat. Soon it would be his turn to speak in front of the class and share what he'd done over the summer.

Stewart felt a sense of dread as his lips tightened into a frown. All he did was go on a boring camping trip. Camping wasn't nearly as exciting as a vacation in New York City.

As Kevin got closer to finishing, Stewart's hands grew sweaty. He bit his lower lip. He didn't know what to tell his classmates. Everything flew from his mind, and no matter how hard he tried, all he got was . . . nothing. He couldn't focus on anything but the sound of his heart beating inside his chest. Thump, thump, thump.

He *hated* speaking in class. He didn't have anything funny or interesting to contribute. His fingers trembled; his stomach lurched just at the thought of it.

What was he going to share? All he could remember was catching one measly fish. Everyone was going to laugh at him.

Stewart's knees shook; he fumbled for a pencil and gripped it in his hands. His knuckles turned white. The class erupted in applause for Kevin's story.

"Well, Kevin," Mrs. Ort said. "That was certainly a wonderful way to spend the summer. Stewart, please come up."

Stewart looked at all the kids in the class. He sat, glued to his seat. Closing his eyes, he clutched his stomach and said in a small voice, "I have to go to the bathroom." The students stirred restlessly. He didn't want to talk in front of the class. He knew they'd laugh and make fun of him. Stewart lowered his head.

Mrs. Ort nodded; Stewart stood, grabbed a hall pass, and stumbled from the room.

jasmine's ideas for coping with anxiety

anchor breathing

Public speaking can be hard, but I have an awesome trick. Right before I go on stage, or into the game, or in front of the class, I think it's helpful and fun to do "anchor breathing." Imagine yourself on a boat or raft, feeling safe and content there on the water. Picture an anchor attached to your boat, keeping you right there in that happy place. Just like an anchor on a boat keeps it from floating away, our own bodies have anchor spots that can help us feel grounded and safe. One anchor spot is at our core—our belly. Another is at our nose and mouth, and my favorite is at the chest and lungs. So try this: Place your hands in the middle of your chest and breathe in deeply. Then exhale slowly. Feel the rise and fall of your ribs as you inhale and release. You don't even have to use your hands. Anchor spots are free and always available—give one a try next time you're feeling nervous!

i spy my strong self

When I have to give a presentation at school, I sometimes feel super anxious. Even though I have done the work and put in loads of time practicing, I still need this exercise to help me feel more confident. It's called visual imagery. Picturing myself feeling strong and prepared can help me feel more positive about myself in difficult situations. To do this, I find a quiet place to sit and close my eyes. I imagine myself going into the classroom or on stage, wherever I need to be. My head is high. My shoulders are relaxed. I am grinning. I breathe deeply and see my friends smiling back at me. I speak clearly. I can do this!

STORY 7

face-off with a bully

"You played great basketball yesterday," Gabe said. He slid onto a seat at the lunch table next to Matt. Matt was the best basketball player in the school. He was taller than the other kids and had great moves. Gabe wanted to hang out with him, but Matt usually treated him like he didn't really want him there.

"Move," Matt said loud enough that people sitting at the next table heard. "Don't sit so close to me." Gabe shifted in his seat, his eyes downcast. He slid farther away. Matt said, "That's not far enough."

Gabe thought about moving, but his feet felt glued to the floor. If he moved, everybody would talk about it. Instead, he raised his water bottle to take a drink. He watched Matt from the corner of his eye. As he swallowed too fast, he choked on the liquid.

Everyone at the table snickered. Matt scowled back at him, then turned his back on Gabe, facing in the other direction.

Gabe wished he could sink out of sight under the table. His cheeks grew warm. He put his hands in his lap; his shoulders sagged. He shrugged as if he didn't care, but he really *did* care. Sighing deeply, Gabe was silent. He fidgeted with the plastic wrap of his sandwich, not even hungry anymore.

Matt turned to him and said, "You should really leave. This table is for the team."

Gabe swallowed. "There's no sign saying this is your table."

"Really?" Matt snarled. He lashed out, pushing Gabe's sandwich so it landed on the floor.

"That's my sandwich," Gabe said, his voice small. He sat frozen in his seat, his legs feeling like lead. His shoulders caved inward. Should he pick up his sandwich? *Walk away?* He wished he could become invisible and disappear. He looked up, his face tight with shame. He didn't want to be there anymore.

 ## colby's tricks for dealing with negative behavior

so many parts!

If I get picked on, I sometimes feel bad about myself. It's hard when someone else's behavior makes me feel this way—I feel like embarrassment has taken over my whole body. But when I get embarrassed, this technique helps. I use it to remind myself of everything I am. Yes, I tell myself that I feel embarrassed, but I am not just embarrassment. I feel mad, but I am not just anger. I list all the other things that I am *also*. I am *also* kind and thoughtful. I am sad *and* happy. I am brave *and* loving. I am artistic *and* unique. I am not just one thing. Recognizing my many parts helps me feel better and more mindful of all that I am.

response versus reaction

When someone says or does something to make me feel bad, I can react quickly. Sometimes I've cried, yelled, or even thrown or kicked things. Some of these reactions happened without me thinking about it. But the Mindful Me can help me choose my response. When I tune in to my thinking brain and the hippocampus (the area that remembers things), I can make a plan so I will react in a better way so later I won't wish I had done things differently. When I get upset, but then pause and breathe, my hippocampus switches on and reminds me what can happen when I react too quickly. I can play out a scene in my head and choose a different, better response.

STORY 8

erica's homework horrors

Erica was staring at her homework, chewing on a pencil, when she cracked the metal at the end of the eraser. "Erica!" her mother yelled. "Stop that!"

"Can I watch TV?" Brady asked.

"Did you finish your homework?" her mom asked her brother.

"Done!" Brady held up his math assignment. Mom nodded.

Erica sighed, then heard the TV blasting from the den. Her eyes narrowed; she felt cheated. Erica was jealous. She wanted to watch TV, too. She looked at her worksheet, her eyes heavy. She wouldn't finish in time for her favorite show. When she looked at the math examples, she had no idea how to proceed.

"Hurry, Erica. Dinner is in 10 minutes," she heard her mom say. Erica's stomach churned. She shook her leg nervously. She pulled out another pencil. She erased her answers, rubbing the eraser so hard the paper ripped.

"Erica! What are you doing?" Mom walked over to the drawer and grabbed some tape to repair the paper. Erica watched, her hands in her lap, her shoulders sagging. She turned and looked into the den at her brother sprawled on the couch. Brady was so smart. He knew all the answers. He never had to ask for help.

Erica's throat was clogged, and her eyes stung. She was frustrated and didn't want to be in the kitchen; she wanted to watch TV. With jerky movements, she yanked her bag open and grabbed another pencil. She looked at the math problem again, her eyes squeezed tightly together, but all she could think about was Brady on the couch watching *her* favorite show in five minutes.

That's it, Erica thought, and stuffed her unfinished homework into her bag.

"I didn't check it," Mom said.

"That's okay," Erica answered, her face red. "I know it's right."

zeke's ideas for when you're feeling overwhelmed

take five

"Take Five" is a great exercise when I am feeling overwhelmed. In this activity, you can pretend you're a detective. Begin with your eyes closed. Listen for five different sounds. Some might be inside, some outside, and you might even hear the sound of your own quiet breathing. Then notice five things that you can feel on your own body. Notice the warmth of your hands, the texture of your clothes, the pressure of your back against the chair. Then slowly open your eyes and look for five things around you that you hadn't noticed before. This exercise will reset your mind. Now, you will be calm enough to tell your mom why you are frustrated—and maybe get some help for that annoying homework!

broaden your horizons

Feeling frustrated and confused can make your whole mind feel trapped. You may feel like you're NEVER going to understand. When this happens to me, I do a mindfulness trick. Here's what you do: Go outside, or to a window, and look straight out into the distance, to the farthest point you can see. Look to the right and to the left, like an explorer at sea. Expand your gaze in every direction. Challenge your brain to take in new information, and feel intense emotions start to fade. When you do this, your world becomes bigger than just your problem at the moment. Not only that, but the pathways in your brain are opened now, and your mind becomes more ready for learning!

how to be totally mindful

kayli's lesson: being mindful every day

An important part of being mindful is noticing what is going on around you, or even in your own body or mind, without labeling it good or bad—just noticing. I like to think of myself as a scientist who is always interested in studying something fascinating—me! I practice observing myself. When I'm walking, I feel my feet on the ground. When I'm eating, I pay attention to the tastes in my mouth.

Being mindful when you are upset is noticing that you are feeling sad or angry or frustrated or jealous. Are your shoulders hunched? Are your hands clenched? Do you feel sick to your stomach? Being mindful when you are happy is the same thing—it's paying attention to your feelings of joy or comfort or love. Is your back straight? Are your arms lifted? Does your heart feel light and open? Sometimes you are relaxed, or thirsty, or fidgety. See if you can experience these sensations without thinking of them as good or bad. They are just comfort or thirst or twitchiness.

Practicing mindfulness means noticing what is going on in your life from moment to moment without judgment. You are aware. You are awake. You are mindful, and this can help you in everything you do!

STORY 9

chelsea trips up in baseball

The baseball game began, and everybody was cheering. Chelsea was the first batter up to the plate. Her eyes found her father, who smiled at her. She heard the encouraging yells of the coach and watched with rising excitement as the pitcher wound up her arm.

The ball flew toward her. With a grimace, she watched it head toward her and fought the surge of panic as well as the impulse to duck. The ball whizzed past her cheek; she smiled when the umpire shouted, "Ball!"

She heard clapping from her side of the field. The pitcher stepped forward; the ball was spinning toward her again.

Chelsea's father yelled, "Bend your knees!" She looked toward the left where the voice came from, and the ball struck her on the hip. Chelsea's left leg collapsed beneath her; she went down like

41

a sack of flour. Gasping, she grabbed her side, her skin burning under her uniform. Blinking back tears of embarrassment, she fought to keep her lips from trembling. The coach was bending down, and Chelsea heard her father's concerned voice ask if she was okay.

Hands touched her side, but she brushed them impatiently away. *This is so embarrassing*, she thought. Chelsea wished the ground would open up so she could fall into the biggest hole until she was sure she wouldn't cry. She turned her face into her shoulder, trying to control her shaking body.

Taking a deep breath, she forced herself to stand and turned her tight lips into a wobbly smile. Her face was flushed, and she felt sweat running off her skin.

Chelsea looked over at her teammates, a blush spreading up into her face. She waved like the players on television do to show she was okay, even though inside she felt a hot rush of embarrassment. She said nothing. She didn't trust words to come out of her mouth without sobbing.

kayli's suggestions for handling embarrassment and frustration

labeling, labeling

Have you ever felt embarrassed in front of other people? When that happens to me, I like to focus on myself, rather than on everybody else's reactions. I pay attention to what is happening to me physically at that moment, and then I label it. I feel my face growing hot and red, so I say inside myself, "Burning, burning." I notice my heart racing: "Pounding, pounding." I see my fists clenching: "Tightening, tightening." I sense the soles of my feet on the floor: "Standing, standing." When I label my experience with a name, it doesn't feel so overwhelming—and it helps me overcome the embarrassing situation, too!

mental body scan

Disappointment is a feeling I notice when things don't go the way I had hoped. In my head I might blame myself or others. Doing a "mental body scan" helps me pay attention to my body as it is right now and stop reliving what happened in the past. Here's how: Start at your feet. Notice their position. Relax your stomach muscles, and notice the rise and fall of your rib cage as you breathe. Relax your shoulders. Notice the weight of your arms. Where are your hands resting? Open and close your mouth. What does your face feel like? How about the top of your head? Paying close attention to yourself and what is happening in your own body can help you relax, and it can help make your problems seem a little further away and not so big.

STORY 10

ryan gets in deep trouble

"You think a broken window is funny, Ryan?" demanded his teacher, Mr. Stephens.

Ryan took a step backward, shaking his head. He opened his mouth to murmur, "No." *Mr. Stephens looks really mad*, Ryan thought. He looked around. Isabelle had moved far to the right of him. Chase had disappeared altogether. *They were both here a minute ago when we were playing*, he thought.

Ryan never meant to hit the window! He wanted to tell Mr. Stephens that, but the words wouldn't come out. He stuttered for a second, then clamped his mouth shut and stared at the broken glass.

He looked around the playground, his stomach starting to feel funny when he realized he was standing alone. All the kids had moved far away from him. Ryan's knees shook. He looked for Chase and saw him over by the water fountain.

It was very quiet in the schoolyard; he couldn't hear the squeaking of the swings or the bouncing balls. His face lost all color, and he felt dizzy when he looked back at the teacher towering over him. Ryan felt the air leaving his lungs; he couldn't suck in another breath. His lower lip trembled; he suddenly needed to go to the bathroom, badly. Really badly. He hopped from one foot to the other.

"Didn't I tell you kids not to throw the ball at the building?"

Ryan whimpered and looked up at him. He opened his mouth to say it was an accident, but the only thing that came out was a choked whisper.

"It wasn't me," Isabelle called from a distance.

"If it wasn't you, Isabelle, then who threw the ball?" the teacher's eyes narrowed as he looked at Ryan. Ryan felt weak; he started breathing fast. His head had an empty feeling. What was going to happen to him, he wondered. Tears prickled his eyes. *What do they do to students who break things in school?*

willow's tips for dealing with anxiety

belly breathing

Have you ever felt like Ryan? Here's a great idea for when you are feeling anxious: Direct your attention to your "core"—your stomach muscles. As you breathe in, let your stomach expand like a balloon. Then, as you breathe out, use your stomach muscles to pull your belly button back toward your backbone. Notice how your stomach grows and shrinks with each full breath. Expanding and contracting can help you center your body *and* your mind. If you want, you can place your hand on your stomach to help keep your attention there. You can use this trick to feel better in a crowded place, or at home alone!

do the opposite

Sometimes it helps me to notice *where* I am feeling my emotions. When I want to cry, I feel stinging in my eyes or a lump in my throat. When I'm frustrated, I might notice my hands clenching. When I'm nervous, I feel my heart racing. See what is true for you, and then do the opposite. If your throat feels tight, open your jaw wide and swallow. If your heart is beating fast, let out a long, slow breath to slow down your heart rate. You can use your body to send messages to your brain to calm yourself down. Pretty cool, huh?

part three

how to be a mindful you with friends

STORY 11

best friends no more?

Jenna kicked the folded paper to Violet in the next row.

"What's that?" Grace whispered, pointing to the paper. Violet didn't answer as she picked it up. "Violet!" Grace tried to get her best friend's attention.

"Shhhh." Violet held her finger to her lips, then tilted her head toward the teacher.

Grace watched her friend, her mouth turning down into a frown. Something was going on. Grace clenched her pencil. She kept turning to look at Violet and Jenna, who raised their eyebrows and smiled as if they had a great secret.

"See you later," Jenna said so softly that only Grace and Violet heard it.

"Who?" Grace asked with a shrug. Jenna didn't answer her. All she did was giggle again. The answering laugh from Violet made Grace feel left out. Violet was *her* friend! They'd been friends since pre-k. Why was Jenna writing notes to her?

Grace looked for the note. She wanted to read it. Her finger burned to touch it; an alarming thought wormed its way into her head. Grace's throat clogged with fear. She glanced sideways at Violet, who was grinning at Jenna. The bell rang. Everybody gathered their bags and raced for the door. Grace called to Violet, but her friend must not have heard her because she walked off with Jenna.

As Grace made her way to the exit, her feet dragging, she noticed a small piece of paper on the floor. She recognized it. It must have fallen out of Violet's school bag! Grace scooped it up and opened it. "c u l8r" was written in a large scrawl across the page. A tear slipped from her eye. She dashed it away, but her eyes felt heavy with the tears she knew were coming. Her best friend had made a play date, and Grace was jealous; she was not invited.

kayli's suggestions for feeling better

dog-bowl chime

I once spent the whole day feeling bad about something that happened with my friend. When I got home and kicked off my shoes in the mudroom, my sneaker hit my dog's water bowl and let out a beautiful ringing sound. I stood still and listened to the sound until it was completely gone. It was like magic! The best part was, I had forgotten about my bad feelings for 20 seconds and already felt a little better! Try tapping a metal bowl with a wooden spoon at home, and listen quietly until the sound stops. See how you feel. Then feed your pet or do something else that feels good!

open senses

It can really help to move to a different spot when you are feeling crummy. I like to walk slowly away from the area where I got upset. I feel my feet on the ground and then look around. I try to tune in to things around me that I didn't notice before. I ask myself: "What do I see?" "What do I hear?" "Can I smell anything?" I keep all my senses open. If you practice this often, you can get good at noticing things around you even when you feel rotten. It helps me recognize the good stuff, too.

emotions

anger
frustration
overwhelm

STORY 12

you broke my controller!

Kyle and Spencer were locked in a video game race in the den. Kyle was smacking his controller roughly as he played. Suddenly the screen went dark.

Kyle fiddled with the game controller. "Something's wrong."

"Give it to me, Kyle." Spencer tried to snatch the game controller from Kyle's hands. Kyle held it against his chest, keeping it from Spencer's reach.

"No, I've got it," Kyle said.

Spencer pried it from Kyle's hands. He turned to the television, moving the two small buttons with his thumbs. *Nothing: no noise, no clicks.* "What did you do to it? It's not working."

"No way," Kyle responded, reaching out to try to take back the controller. "It was working a few minutes ago."

55

"Well, it's not working now. I can't believe you broke it." Spencer continued to press the small yellow and red buttons. "I just got this. It's brand new."

"You don't know what you're doing," Kyle told him. "I can fix it."

Spencer felt angry and insulted. He knew everything about this game system, and it was *his* new system. He moved closer to the television and pressed the buttons harder. It didn't work. Spencer threw down the controller and crossed his arms in front of himself in a huff. "I think you should go home now," he said to Kyle. His eyes were tiny slits, and he felt himself growing angrier and angrier at Kyle for breaking his controller. He was mad and never wanted to play with Kyle again. He glared at Kyle, "You probably broke it on purpose."

Kyle shouted back "I did not! You probably gave me the one with a problem so you could win. You're a sore loser! I'm a better player than you!"

Spencer's heart beat like the drum he used in marching band. He closed his mouth. He didn't want to talk to Kyle ever again.

jasmine's ideas for calming the mind

mind jar

When I'm full of thoughts and emotions, my mind can whirl around like a crazy tornado. It's hard to think straight when that happens. A "mind jar" can help. Get an empty bottle (I use a plastic drink bottle with the label removed) and fill it almost to the top with water. Then, think of three or four feelings that you have experienced that make your thoughts spin. Then sprinkle in three or four pinches of glitter (any color). Each pinch represents one of those feelings. Close the bottle tightly and shake it up! This is your mind whirling! Now take a mindful moment to

watch the bits of glitter slowly fall in front of your eyes. Breathe deeply as the sparkles settle to the bottom.

turtle pose

Are you ever so upset that you just want to curl up and hide? Turtle pose is great when that happens. Start this yoga move by sitting on your "knees-bottom" (on your knees, but then sitting back so your bottom rests on the backs of your legs). Curl forward until your forehead touches the floor in front of you. Rest your arms beside you, fingers pointing back to your toes. Hey, turtle! Rest here. Relax. Nothing can get to you. You are protected and safe. You are strong and still. Maybe this will be your new favorite calming move!

STORY 13

the not-so-friendly friend

"Hi, Meghan! Your mom let me in." Alexis stood outside Meghan's bedroom.

Meghan was lying on the bed, staring at the ceiling. She reluctantly slipped off the bed and stood there, her arms hanging at her sides.

Alexis ran to a stack of several games on a shelf. "I love this one," she said, pulling down a box.

Meghan shook her head. "I don't want to play that game," she said, shoving the game back into its spot.

Alexis grabbed a pile of coloring books. The tin holding the crayons tipped, spilling them all over the floor. Meghan sighed. She rubbed her eyes. She didn't feel like coloring. She looked at Alexis. She didn't want company. She looked at the door longingly, and put in her headphones, wishing she had never invited Alexis today. It wasn't that she didn't like her; she just wasn't in the mood to play with Alexis right now.

Her friend's face flushed. "What . . . what do you want to do instead?" Meghan opened her mouth but the words stuck in her throat. She didn't know what to say. They had made plans to play so long ago, and it felt okay at the time, but right now, she didn't want to do anything. Alexis was staring at her. Meghan suddenly thought, *What if Alexis gets angry and doesn't want to be my friend anymore? What if she tells everyone she didn't have a good time at my house?*

"We could play a song," Alexis suggested in a low voice.

"Fine," Meghan said, taking out her headphones, but she really didn't want to. "Fine," she repeated as she flopped to the floor and waited for Alexis to turn on the music.

zeke's ideas for speaking up and not taking things personally

"i messages"

In this story, Alexis is confused by Meghan's unfriendly behavior. And Meghan seems pretty miserable, too. When I'm feeling sad or lonely, it can seem impossible to talk to people. Sometimes I try to tune in to "Mindful Me" and check in with what I'm feeling. Then I can give "I messages" to my friend, teacher, or family member and get help. Messages like this: "I feel sad." "I need some time to myself." "I want a turn." "I feel left out." "I need a hug." I can't control anyone else, but I can be truthful and share what I feel and ask for what I need. Both Alexis and Meghan could practice this communication exercise—and so can you. Give it a try!

putting yourself in their shoes

Even people we love can upset us. It can be really hard to imagine thinking good thoughts about someone who acts mean or unkind, but scientists say that when you think kind thoughts, you are happier. Try this activity and see how it works. Find a quiet spot where you feel safe, and close your eyes. Imagine whoever it was who upset you (your friend, brother, sister . . .). See if you can put yourself in their position. Imagine you are  the one who is feeling cranky or frustrated. What would help you in that situation? Think about what they might need. Maybe they could use some personal space, or quiet, or a second chance. Putting yourself in their shoes can help you not take it personally. You can think more clearly and feel better about the whole situation.

you always have a choice

zeke's lesson: using your own power to choose

Every day, things happen to us or around us that we do not choose, and it can make us feel out of control. Something I have learned, but always have to remind myself of, is that the only thing I can control is *me*. So when something happens that I don't like, I try to remember that *I* can control how I respond to it. For example, if I were Alexis, and stuck in a situation where my friend wasn't being nice to me, I would try to remember, *It's not me; it's them.* If exercises like "I Messages" and "Putting Yourself in Their Shoes" don't help, I try to find something else to do—with someone else, if possible. For example, I might ask a parent if there was something I could do to help them. Just being with another friendly person can make you feel better. We can't control others, but we're totally in charge of ourselves!

STORY 14

sore loser

"Did not!"

"Did too!"

"I don't want to play anymore." Chloe threw the playing cards facedown, refusing to show them.

"Girls?" Lily's mom called from the kitchen. "Is there a problem?"

Lily looked at Chloe and bit her lip. Mad as she was that Chloe had cheated again, she didn't want to tell her mother and lose the play date. Grinding her teeth, she answered, "No."

Lily reached for Chloe's cards, turning them over to expose the Old Maid. "You had the Old Maid. I knew you had it. You're a sore loser," Lily whispered angrily.

Chloe tried to speak, but Lily held her hand up, then began piling up the cards, her movements clipped and stiff. She stacked them impatiently, stuffing them back into their box, bending a few of them. This was the second time Chloe had stopped a game when she was losing. "Want to play something else?" Chloe finally asked.

"No," Lily answered shortly. The more she thought about it, the more she wished Chloe would just go home and not come back. Lily glanced at the clock and wouldn't look at her friend. Sometimes Chloe acted like such a baby.

Lily finished cleaning up the cards, then threw herself back on the couch with exasperation. She watched Chloe sitting there pouting. Her friend's brows were lowered, and the sniffs were coming faster.

Lily made a noise, like a hum, to show Chloe she was still mad. This only made Chloe stifle a sob. Lily folded her hands across her stomach, making her lips form a grim line. She made that noise again to let Chloe know she wasn't happy with her. She kept her chin pointed upward, just like Mom did when she was angry.

Chloe walked over slowly and sat next to her. "Nobody ever lets me win at my house," she said sadly. "My brother cheats all the time, and I just wanted to win today."

Lily scooted far away, then glared at her. "You know, someone's gotta lose," she told her.

willow's advice on finding mindful balance

tree pose

When I'm upset, I try "mindful movement." Here is one of my favorite yoga moves. Begin a "tree pose" by standing tall, holding your hands together in front of you, and reaching your arms to the sky. Then spread your arms and fingers like branches, and shift your weight onto one leg. Keep your gaze on one spot in front of you. Slowly lift the other leg and bring your foot to the inside of your standing leg, right above the calf. (You can lean on a wall with one hand to help.) Balance and breathe. Then bring your leg and hands down slowly, and repeat on the other side.

mindful listening

It feels nice when someone really listens to what you have to say, right? Here's how you can practice mindful listening when someone is telling *you* something. Don't say anything at first—just listen. As you listen, notice the person's face. Can you tell what emotion they might be feeling? Look at their body movements. Are they open and happy, or scrunched up and mad? Give them eye contact.

Listen to their words, but don't offer your own ideas unless they ask for them. Don't tell your own story. Just be there, nodding or smiling. Notice how you feel as they talk. Pay attention to how you move your own body as you sit there. Sometimes you'll realize you both are sitting the same way! When you practice listening this way, you are on your way to making good connections with others and being a great listener.

STORY 15

losing her best friend

Hannah sat on her front step with her knees up and her chin resting on her knees. The sun was up and shining brightly, but it didn't matter. She sighed heavily. She should never have gotten out of bed. She was feeling very sad.

Next door, the moving van had already arrived. It was real: Molly was leaving. Molly had been her best friend from the time they were two years old. They did *everything* together. Memories filled her head, and Hannah felt her eyes sting with tears. She loved Molly. They had shared so many secrets. They had played the same games. *Nobody is as much fun as my friend*, Hannah thought sadly.

A big tear plopped on the step. Hannah sniffled. She had promised her mother she wasn't going to cry, but she couldn't help it. She rested her cheek on her knee. She closed her eyes and told herself not to cry. She breathed heavily through her nose. Just then, Molly opened her screen door. She waved happily at Hannah.

Hannah raised her hand. It felt too heavy to lift it. She sniffled loudly, and Molly skipped over.

Molly sat down next to her, offering Hannah a cookie. Hannah looked at the tasty treat. They were her favorites, and Molly's mom had made them especially for Hannah. *I'm never going to eat them again*, Hannah thought unhappily. She bit into the chocolate chip cookie; her mouth was dry. These cookies usually tasted delicious. She chewed and took another bite. Nope, it was still tasteless.

Hannah looked at Molly and opened her mouth, but no words came out. Molly touched her shoulder and said, "Don't worry, Hannah. We'll call each other every day." Hannah knew Molly was saying that to make her feel better, but all it did was make her feel worse. It was truly the worst day of her life.

 colby's thoughts on building resiliency

notice and name

Resiliency is inner strength. It's feeling better again after you've been upset. Even when you feel completely defeated, there are things you can do to help yourself feel strong again. Imagine all your emotions are in your backpack. Sometimes your load gets so heavy that you need to slow down and unpack it so you can move on. When this happens, stop whatever you are doing and imagine yourself taking off your backpack. Unzip it. What do you notice? Does anger burst out? Can you picture sadness scrunched up in the back pocket? Does frustration swirl out in a cloud of smoke? Is disappointment heavy at the bottom? Name each of your feelings as you become aware of them. The first step to feeling lighter is to notice and name what is weighing you down.

gratitude list

I keep a list on my wall of things that I am thankful for. I add to it whenever I notice something great in my life. It can be hard to remember that even when things are not going well, there are still good things in the world. If I'm upset but am ready to move on, I make a list of eight things that I am grateful for—they could be about my day, my friendships, my family, or myself. Try making a gratitude list for yourself, or one for your whole family. Add to it, and every time you read it, your heart will feel better. That feeling better part is called resiliency—you've gotten through a hard time, and you can still connect with all the good things out there!

keep mindfulness going

jasmine's lesson: make a gratitude and intention list

So now you know about mindfulness and how it can help you. How do you keep the mindfulness going? With reminders, of course! Here's how:

Start a gratitude list, just like in the previous exercise. You can use a piece of paper, a notebook, or a dry-erase board. Put the list somewhere where you will see it often, like on the kitchen counter or on the wall outside the bathroom. Each day, add one or two things that you are thankful for, maybe things that made you smile or laugh or feel better that day. Keep a list for your whole family. You can *all* add to it. When it gets full, maybe at the end of the month, take a picture of it or save it somewhere special and start a new page.

Now, each time you write down something good, you can set an "intention" for the days and weeks ahead. An intention is like a promise. You might have an intention like "Notice kindness" or "Remember to breathe." Keep your intention in your mind and heart.

At the end of the year, get out all those old gratitude lists and read them together. Then you and your family can set

Gratitude

1. I am grateful for my family.

2. I am grateful for my friends.

3. I am grateful for warm sunshine.

Intentions

1. Remember to take deep breaths when I feel upset.

2. Smile more and frown less.

3. Try a mindfulness exercise when I feel really sad, mad, or angry.

your intentions for the next year—just like resolutions, but mindful ones!

Being mindful, as you now know, can help you in so many ways, and it can make life more fun. When you pay attention to the world, all the people around you, and yourself, you make more connections. You are present and awake and tuned in to the world. You are aware of everything around you, and you are able to make great choices!

how to learn more about mindfulness

for children

Aldefer, Lauren. *Mindful Monkey, Happy Panda*. Somerville, MA: Wisdom Publications, 2011.

The two friends in this story guide readers in demonstrating how to be mindful from one moment to the next as they go about their busy lives.

Davies, Candice L. *Tini and Rhogi Yogini and Yogi: An Introduction to Kids' Yoga and DharmaDinos*. Indianapolis: Dog Ear Publishing, 2016.

DharmaDinos provides tools that support parents, therapists, and teachers in bringing yoga and mindfulness into homes and classrooms (DharmaDinos.net).

Harris, Angie. *Mad to Glad: Simple Lessons to Help Children Cope with Changing Emotions*. Mindful Aromatherapy, LLC, 2015. (Available in Spanish and English.)

This children's book contains fun and interactive mindfulness lessons to increase focusing abilities and bring awareness to a range of feelings.

MacLean, Kerry Lee. *Moody Cow Meditates*. Somerville, MA: Wisdom Publications, 2009.

This book serves as a terrific introduction to meditation for children. "Mind Jar" recipe included!

Muth, Jon J. *The Three Questions*. New York: Scholastic Press, 2002.

Based on the original by Leo Tolstoy, this beautifully illustrated children's book reminds readers of all ages of what is most important in this world as they question how to spend their time, choose their actions, and interact with one another.

GoNoodle.com is a great resource with mindfulness-based activities for kids.

CommonSenseMedia.org/lists/meditation-apps-for-kids has many great apps to help kids learn about mindfulness.

for adults and adolescents

Dalai Lama and Desmond Tutu, with Douglas Abrams. *The Book of Joy*. New York: Penguin Publishing Group, 2016.

Esile, Lisa and Franco Esile. *Whose Mind Is It Anyway? Get out of Your Head and into Your Life*. New York: TarcherPerigee, 2016.

Hanh, Thich Nhat. *The Miracle of Mindfulness*. Boston: Beacon Press, 1996.

Kabat-Zinn, Jon. *Mindfulness for Beginners: Reclaiming the Present Moment and Your Life*. Boulder, CO: Sounds True. 2012.

Lelord, Francois. *Hector and the Search for Happiness*. New York: Penguin Books, 2010. (Also a 2014 film.)

about the authors

 **Carole P. Roman** is the award-winning author of more than 50 children's books. Whether about pirates, princesses, or discovering the world around us, her books have enchanted educators, parents, and her diverse audience of children. She writes both fiction and non-fiction, from verse to chapter books for all age groups. She hosts three blog radio programs and is one of the founders of a new magazine, *Indie Author's Monthly*. She's been interviewed twice by *Forbes* magazine. Carole has co-authored (with Julie A. Gerber) a self-help book, *Navigating Indieworld: A Beginners Guide to Self-Publishing and Marketing*, as well as an adult fiction book under the pen name Brit Lunden. She lives on Long Island. Her series include *Captain No Beard, If You Were Me and Lived in* (Cultural), *If You Were Me and Lived in* (Historical), a nursery series, and *Oh Susannah* (early reader).

You can learn more about Carole P. Roman by visiting her blog, caroleproman.blogspot.com, or her website, CarolePRoman.com.

 **J. Robin Albertson-Wren** has been teaching elementary-age children for more than 20 years in Charlottesville, Virginia. She is a mother, classroom teacher, workshop leader, public speaker, and certified mindfulness instructor through Mindful Schools. Her passion is teaching mindfulness techniques to executives, educators, parents, adolescents, and children.

Visit MindAwake at Mind-Awake.Weebly.com to learn more.

CPSIA information can be obtained
at www.ICGtesting.com
Printed in the USA
BVHW021540040620
580765BV00009B/104

9 781641 520850